DUST
In the
Strom

Abha Kala

DUST IN THE STORM

Abha Kala

BLACK EAGLE BOOKS
Dublin, USA | Bhubaneswar, India

 Black Eagle Books
USA address:
7464 Wisdom Lane
Dublin, OH 43016

India address:
E/312, Trident Galaxy, Kalinga Nagar,
Bhubaneswar-751003, Odisha, India

E-mail: info@blackeaglebooks.org
Website: www.blackeaglebooks.org

First International Edition Published by
Black Eagle Books, 2024

DUST IN THE STORM
by **Abha Kala**

Copyright © Abha Kala

All rights reserved. No part of this publication may be reproduced, stored in a retrieval system, or transmitted, in any form or by any means, electronic, mechanical, photocopying, recording or otherwise without the prior permission of the publisher.

Distribution in **India by Pralek Prakashan**

Cover & Interior Design: Ezy's Publication

ISBN- 978-1-64560-605-5 (Paperback)
Library of Congress Control Number: 2024950957

Printed in the United States of America

To,

Debashis, Radhika, Siddhant

Preface

Dear Readers,
I am thrilled as well as a little hesitant to venture into the realm of publishing my first English language poetry compilation. It is like taking my first baby step. The compilation 'Dust in the storm' is simple as well as philosophical. It has altogether thirty-two poems representing the different stops on the journey of my life. They are the manifestation of my dreams and aspirations, encompassing memories from childhood and my life in adulthood. I have always believed that poetry is one of the best and most powerful medium to express even mundane things with profundity, in few words. It is never easy to write something sublime and thought provoking with brevity; but poetry allows such direct communication. This is the beauty of poetry.

I appreciate life and am always in awe of this beautiful world. This is the reason my poems are full of optimism even when its subjects are complex. Topics like love, sleep, and death, though common, may not have similar impact on all people. I hope to share my stories with you through this book. The poems:

'Death', 'Me and My Mirror', 'The Solitary Walk', 'Ode to Sleep', 'A Call', 'The Spirits'- are philosophical in nature.

'Realisation' and 'Ode to Unrequited Love' are about my dreams and quests. Some poems fall in the category of nostalgia, like- 'The Tamarind Tree', 'Ode to loneliness'; while some explore my deep bond with nature. Nature is God's manifestation. It is not only beautiful but also very mysterious. It has always acted like a healer for me; imbuing me with sublime serenity and inspiration. My visit to Kailash Mansarovar further strengthened this bond; it not only humbled me, but changed my perspective on life. 'My Basket is Full' speaks about this experience.

I do not boast that these poems are literary marvels. Nor would I like you to read them in that spirit. Rather, these poems are just me depicting my pleasures, dreams and uncertainties in a way that makes me happy. I hope you enjoy them and my simple words can inspire you to share your stories as well. Thanks,

Abha Kala

Contents

Preface 07

The Solitary Walk 11
The God's Abode 12
You and me 14
Musing! 15
Common Man 17
Imperfectly Perfect 19
Realisation! 20
My Wish 21
How to Live 23
Dilemma Solved 25
A Call! 26
Enigma 27
Me and My Mirror 29
Nature and Me 31
The Child 33
The Folly of Love 35
If Death! 37
My Basket is Full 39
The ashes collected 41
The Spirits 43
Ode to Loneliness 46
Acquaintance. 48
To undo. 50

Enamoured 51
Radha of Krishna 53
Ode to Unrequited Love 54
Martyrs 57
The Tamarind Tree 59
Ode to Sleep 61
Hope 64
The Sea and Me 66
The Clouds 68
May I Be 70
My Journey 71
Who ? 73

The Solitary Walk

Something is missing.
It seems my soul has gone for a long walk.
Listening to birds' song.
Wind's chatter.
Drinking the water of sparkling springs.
Touching the snow of iced-caped
mountains with hands.
Running in the white sand beaches.
Giggling in the meadows of hillside.
Eating the berries and wild fruits
from the eternal garden of blessings.
I think my soul is finally free to bask
in sunshine.
The long walk brings a strange felicity.

The God's Abode

The woods were silent.
The trees were standing uncomfortably close.
There was no space.
I felt a little breathlessness.
An intimacy was missing.
Replica of humanity.
It was as if each stood as sentinel for other.
The rustling of leaves was inaudible.
The sun rays were making desperate effort to sneak inside.
The woods appeared dark and deep.
Oblivious of their existence, like forgotten civilizations.
As if generations were buried there.
And have resurfaced from
their graves after a long peaceful sleep.
I felt a chilling sensation in my being.
As if unperceived spirits were roaming freely.
They looked suspiciously at me.
Was it curiosity or indifference?
I was unable to fathom.
The stillness was intense.

Slowly,
Peace descended
Enveloping me.
'Is this the abode of Gods?'
My brain enquired.
Far from the maddening noise.
And my heart whispered,
'*Yes*'.
It is everywhere.
The high mountains.
The vast meadows.
Gurgling rivers.
The silent woods.
All have strange energies.
No doubt.
They are worshipped and revered by mankind.
The beautiful and ecstatic nature is the abode of all Gods.
It is humans who have drawn boundaries of religion, cast, creed.
The sublime is clueless.

You and me

If I become you and you become me.
If both remain in state of flux.
Changing robes whenever needed.
We both will be in a state of bliss.
You could understand better my follies.
I would appreciate your nagging concerns.
You could fathom what things move me.
I could analyse your restlessness.
If I become you and you become me.
Both would be perfect.
You would not complain.
I too would accept you as.
I would know your love.
You would feel my love.
I will take your pains.
You take my blessings.
Both will have abundance to enjoy.

Musing!

The architect surveyed my dilapidated house and said
"*don't worry, I will remove all unnecessary walls and panels.*"
"*The house will look as new.*"
I mused!
If only someone could remove the walls and panels of
despair, hatred, and jealousy,
the inner house too will become beautiful.
The packers stormed my place and cleared the mess within
hours, stacking all objects, neatly piled.
I mused!
If only the mess of hurtful memories, bad relationships,
and grievances could be stored neatly,
so much time and energies could be saved.
The gardener mowed the grass,
removed the weeds, pruned the flower beds.
It looked beautiful with blooming flowers and chirping birds.
I mused!
If only the self becomes a garden and blooms with colourful
flowers and melody,
life will become purposeful.

The night is dark and starry.
Stars are twinkling merrily as if winking.
The moon keeps changing its shape and size.
It appears ethereal.
I mused!
If only one can shine even in darkness of life and spread light of hope and cheer,
the journey of life will become worthwhile.

Common Man

I am a common man.
Neither received any accolades nor the brickbats.
Neither fought nor was fought back.
Always worked with all sincerity,
Yet was never considered worthy.
I am miscellaneous personified.
An epitome of all those who have no name.
You can address me as a farmer, labourer, mason, carpenter,
etc, etc.
I have nothing worthwhile at hand.
At the mercy of influential brethren I thrive.
I am beyond being civilised.
Though aware of my duties, not of my rights.
Lately people have started noticing me.
They gather and raise their voice,
whenever some misfortune strikes me.
They discuss my plight in debates and
meetings.
But now I know the real intention behind
this verbal facade.

I know I am the common man.
My life will remain unchanged.
But my sufferings will help some to climb the ladder of fame.

Imperfectly Perfect

I am imperfectly perfect.
Are we all not?
But I have no qualms.
I am an introverted extrovert.
I love water but not the sea.
I love rivers, those that flow unhindered through the mountains. Summers are good.
Winters are beautiful if sunny.
Dark wintry nights appear solemn to me.
I hate high rise buildings but love the balconies.
I think I am imperfectly perfect as are my choices in life.
I love laughter but hate lies.
I follow intelligent people but not the shrewd.
I like innocence even if it adorns fools.
I love the hue and shades of all colours.
The pastels, as well as the glaring, shocking, and dark.
I love the new-borns with their soft pink lips and hands, along with the old, with their sagging skin and toothless jaw.
I am imperfectly perfect.

Realisation!

I looked at the image of my inner body.
Nothing impressive.
Zigzag bones, skull, and tilted spine.
Throughout life we are bothered about
the outer looks.
Big eyes, sculpted nose, pouted lips, high cheekbones.
Manicured and pedicured hands and feet.
Without realising the intricacies of the body machine.
The inner structure was scary.
I was told your spine has changed;
the bones are becoming weak.
I looked at my face.
It was glowing with extra dose of highlighters and creams.
I realised I was too busy caring for my face and feet.
Without realising they are secondary.
Ultimate truth is the health of spine and bones.
The peace of mind and robust heart.

My Wish

I try my best not to share my fears, my grief, my sorrows,
with people I am close.
Yes.
I don't want them to get into the cauldron of uncertainties
galore. I don't want to appear timid and anxious.
I love my people too much to show that I also lose balance.
I firmly believe spreading joy, fun, and happiness increases it
in abundance.
I believe sharing pain and restlessness do not decrease it.
I believe it is better to shut yourself for some time if you are
hurt or angry or guilty.
Let it pass and you will be moulded back into serenity.
I never believe I am always right but I believe the decisions I
take at any particular situation should never be regretted.
No one is flawless.
No one is a saint.
I neither want to be that.
I just pray and wish I remain human.
Life is like a bubble.
It should be lived with grace and dignity.

I wish my two feeble hands always remain strong to hold someone if need be. This is what I crave.
This is what all I want from this beautiful life.

How to Live

A faint voice surreptitiously echoed!
Stop worrying about life.
Wisdom has taught me it is futile.
Start living. Start enjoying.
Start conversations with your inner self.
"*How?*"
I enquired.
Don't heed to people who always spit
venom.
Don't talk to people who never see any good in anyone.
Stop following those who only search faults if not to their liking.
Try to maintain distance with people who are always judge-mental.
Spend time with happy creatures you will find in abundance in nature Seek those who accept you as you are.
All those who are querulous, disparage you,
Are acrimonious, should be kept apart.
Life is short and beautiful.
It is not meant to be lived pessimistically with grievances.

Smile and laugh liberally so that people look forward to be with you.

Remember you are not dead wood.

Be uncomplicated.

Believe me, to be pure and simple is blessing in disguise.

This you will realise as years pass by.

Dilemma Solved

I tried to live life with purpose.
Now I want to live wild.
I have spent many years trying to find reason.
Now I want to live unreasonably.
I tried to make everyone happy.
Now I want to make myself happy.
I had thought I am indispensable.
I realised lately no person is.
Someone takes your place and life moves on.
I used to think it will be many years before I will grow old.
I realised time flies and before one realises one becomes old.
I would always make list of things I have to do.
Now I have discontinued this practise.
I just live every moment.
This wisdom generally comes late.
But nevertheless, if it comes one should celebrate.
I have got over my anxieties and fears.
I am happy at just being as I am.

A Call!

Don't celebrate me after death.
Love me and hold me while I am alive.
Don't shed tears when I am gone.
Let's laugh together loud till the tears come out while I am still around.
Don't write an epitaph on my grave.
Write for me a love poem when I am still awake.
Let's let go of all our stubbornness and bickering.
And go back to those summers when we were children.
Let's forgo our egos and pride.
Let's be in unison.
Unguent and anoint me with your praise.
Cuddle me till I am erased.
Fill my soul with warmth.
Let me live like a wild flower.
Let us dance in the rain
And soak ourself with dirt and mud.
I doubt people meet after death.
So why not live this life to its fullest.

Enigma

She released her long tresses.
And took a vow!
Not to tie them till the wrong,
done to her is redeemed.
The irony!
She was the princess.
Wife of five brothers.
Close friend of Krishna the saviour.
Still, she felt helpless!
The mute spectators did nothing that
fateful day.
To save her honour and pride.
And it is believed,
She was the main cause of the epic war.
The Pandavas won the Mahabharat war and redeemed
Draupadi's pledge.
But at a great cost.
Thousands died including Draupadi's five sons.
History still does not know how to define Draupadi.
Draupadi the crusader!

Draupadi the fighter!
Draupadi the most strong-willed woman!
Or Draupadi the victim of traditions, politics, ego.
She was never asked!
She was commanded.
She only wanted Arjun with whom she had tied the knot.
She loved him the most.
But fate tied her with all the brothers.
She wanted to live like a queen.
Instead had to spent major part of her life in forests.
Draupadi was like any other girl of that age and times.
But fate moulded her to become the unusual
To be remembered for posterity.
One has to pay a huge price.
Draupadi will forever remain an enigma.

Me and My Mirror

Me and my mirror have a long association.
We shared a good rapport.
For years it always spoke the truth.
It appreciated and admired me.
Gave me smiles and hugs.
Assuaged my sagging ego.
Gave me strength to fight back.
But lately it has changed.
Has become grumpy.
Has been giving me cold vibes.
Why this haggard look?
Is it because of age?
It has lost its lustre and shine.
Maybe the life's turmoil has made it a cynic.
I am unable to find any plausible reason
For this changed demeanour.
I am still the same dame.
Over enthusiastic and conscious.
I know now.
The mirror has lived long.

Has become irritable and touchy.
What to do?
I cannot throw it away.
Too many memories are enshrined.
I think I should search for a new piece
which shows me the way I am.

Nature and Me

Staying in a metropolitan city.
In a high-rise building.
It seems as if I hang in the air.
Every object looks small from up here.
I watch the world from my balcony window.
The distant sea and its myriad moods
Kites soaring high with ease
The cluster of trees laden with flowers
The sound of falling raindrops
Sometimes!
I feel the soothing touch of
rustling breeze on my naked arms
and face.
The shining moon looks as if it is smiling at me.
Eager to engage me in a deep conversation.
The starry night looks pretty and perfect.
But, Alas!
I miss the Earth and its earthy smell.
The feel of it in my palms and soles.
I want to hold all things which the Earth beholds.

I want to walk on grass bare feet.
I want to touch it gently.
My only wish
To be entangled with fallen leaves and flowers
And be buried underneath that.

The Child

I looked at the newly born,
just untied by the umbilical cord.
The bond of all these months.
These nine months were full of varied emotions.
Happiness, pain and anxiety.
The baby opened the eyes,
gave a big yawn.
And went back to sleep.
I hesitatingly touched,
baby's tender hands and feet.
Gratitude overwhelmed me
The bundle of joy was mine.
I have become the creator and protector of the child.
I thanked Almighty profusely.
Promised to look after thee.
Reiterated I will let the child live the way it wants
But as years passed, I became more and more possessive.
I started giving my advice on even those issues which were
not of my concern.
I started having the notion

The child is mine and should follow my dreams.
I would fret, fume and grieve.
Would show my emotions to extreme.
I forgot I had promised to let the child live the way it wants.
I forgot I am just a medium.
I forgot I am just a guide.
I forgot every child should see its own dreams and decide.
I forgot I have to be tender and strong.
I have to help, not to manipulate.
I forgot every child is the father of man.
But now I am at peace.
I have started following my own dreams.

The Folly of Love

I had never envisaged.
Such a tall gentleman,
Would be bulldozed by the short damsel.
She now poked him and was abrasive.
I wonder what went wrong?
The doe eyed and smiling duo
Used to be too picture perfect,
To be true.
Holding hands, they would rave about their love.
They were cynosure of all.
And then the tsunami came.
The misfortune was too much for the dame to handle.
She cajoled the gentleman as if all good in him had vanished. She wanted to break free from his shackles.
His love had become a hindrance.
Realising her need to go,
The gentleman bid her adieu.
She left for green pastures.
Not a word he uttered.
He was shattered.

Turned a loner.
I was just wondering.
For how long love exists.

If Death!

If death is the quest!
To find out about the unknown,
unexplored, onward journey.
Let it come!
Not stealthy like some thief.
Nor it should remain an enigma.
But filled with fun and laughter.
For it is just a change of address of one's residence.
For some from obscurity to fame.
For others from pedestal to bane.
Why to grieve for something
which is going to end in vain.
If death is the only answer to unsolved puzzles and pains,
Let it come!
I will accept it with open arms.
Celebrate it while I am still alive.
Why should one fear thee?
When it is certain it will bless every being.
The waiting is for all.
Usually it knocks the door,

unannounced.
If death is the ultimate truth.
Let it come!
I fancy thee!
Alas! if only I knew,
Where it will take me.

My Basket is Full

I was happy in my cocoon
My trove had various artefacts.
Dried flower petals,
Droplets of grief laden tears,
Torn pages of hidden diary.
Bundles of aged letters,
Neatly tied with an old
faded pink ribbon.
Humming waves of memories.
Few unbelievable dreams.
Soothing lingering fragrance.
Hugs and kisses,
Scattered and ensconced comfortably in one corner.
What more is needed to live?
Me and my basket,
shared a unique bond.
Both of us were in a state of tranquillity.
Now and then,
I would toss and turn the contents of my basket.
It appeared to be full.

However!
Few days back,
Stark truth dawned.
Most of my treasure has
become redundant with time.
Should I discard it?
A strange lightning struck me.
This I, me, mine,
needs to be abandoned.
A little more empathy
and sympathy,
Has to be inculcated.
The unrequited love,
The simmering anger,
The festering hurt,
The cacophony of
false promises,
The embers of jealousy,
The complexity of ego,
All these need to be cremated.

The ashes collected

from the pyre,
Need to be immersed
in the waves of Ganges.
The testimonials
to be kept in the basket.
And ah!
Soon,
The years of regrets.
The years of yearnings.
The years of expectations.
The years of solitude.
Just disappeared.
The new me is now
in deep bliss.
The chanting of Shiva,
the rhythm of Om,
has pervaded my being.
The sound of conch shell,
The beating of drums,
The ringing of bells,

It seems as if,
It was entrenched in me.
Since eternity.
With folded hands,
I offer myself to thee!
Oh! Shiva the creator, Shiva the benefactor, Shiva the destructor Behold me.

The Spirits

"Have you ever met
the spirits?"
I asked the man who works
in the cremation ground.
He looked at me,
with scorn.
And replied,
"I see the corpses,
day in and day out.
I have neither the time,
nor the inclination to
meet the people
who are no more."
It amused me.
We are generally scared
of people who are dead.
Though the one's
who are alive,
Should be more feared.
Do the spirits leave the

body and emerge again,
From the ashes?
Do they also live
like us, the humans?
Though formless and ethereal,
Is the Spirit world more
advanced and divine?
There are multiple questions,
That arise in my mind and
Keeps me preoccupied.
Often, I feel the spirits of
my dear ones who have
left this world long ago,
Guide me to
wade through the
Sea of turbulence.
And help me reach the shores.
On occasion I have seen,
When all doors are closed.
They come to my rescue.
I think spirits are those souls
who are God's messenger.
And help the world invisibly,
In evolution of mankind.
Sometimes it appears as
if my Spirit has left my body.
It conveys to me the message

*"The world is more beautiful,
at other side of eternity."*
One should look at the
world beyond the visible,
with open eyes and mind.
And try to be in unison
with one's soul and divine.

Ode to Loneliness

Oh! dear loneliness,
my companion for life.
I fail to understand,
why do people dread
and detest thee, when you enter their being.
I savour thee.
As you listen to me.
You help me clear the clutter that surrounds my mind.
You never stifle me.
You disabuse me of my follies and faults.
You incarcerate me from my depression.
Oh! dear loneliness,
You show me the path, which I fear to tread.
I, in my imprudence would
have been left a skeptic.
You replenish me with courage and hope.
You prod me to fight my battles with glory.
I look forward to being in your
solemn company.
You help me to connect with

my soul and dormant consciousness.
Oh! dear loneliness,
I revere thee.

Acquaintance.

Somebody enquired,
"Do you know the girl
who is no more?"
"Yes. She was my acquaintance",
The conversation was over.
This is the way
Life proceeds.
There are endless crevices,
Where we fear to tread.
Traces of blood and mud,
We Intercept and circumvent.
Do we really bother,
About worthy things?
Of life's nectar and strings.
Do we perceive the unknown?
Unravel the mysteries galore?
I think we only strive,
Day and night.
To save our being.
Lest it gets trampled.

And crushed by forces unseen.
We ensconce ourselves.
With a sweet lullaby.
Journey continues.
Unabated.
We turn the pages.
Look at the picture
Of empires,
We have built.
And ironically take pride on,
Things which are
Going to perish.
We eat and drink.
Make merry.
But forget.
All those acquaintances,
Which were lost in the milieu.
I sometimes wonder.
If life one day decides,
to give all of us,
One more chance.

To undo.

To rewind, stitch tattered feelings,
Which were lying unattended.
Will sanity rebound?
Realisation will dawn?
Will the chasms,
we had created,
~~Will~~ be filled with sensitivity?
Will we express our
Regrets unabashedly?
Knead the dough of
Life's experiences.
Once again with,
Renewed synergy.
And will acknowledge,
All forgotten acquaintances.
I think! May be
Some will.

Enamoured

The night is starry and bright,
Lit with silver moon and twinkling light.
The wind rustles merrily.
The birds whisper and
whistle sweetly.
The flowers dance and bloom.
The lion and the deer
are seen together.
The air is blissful and serene.
The woods are undoubtedly
in awe.
As if girdled with spirits unseen.
Under the big
Old Oak tree
Doe -eyed
Oblivious of the world,
Someone is sitting alone.
Murmurs are making rounds
She is the one who was
Struck by Cupid's arrow.

But there are neither
traces of injury
nor of pain.
Her demeanour looks ecstatic.
As if she had drank
some magic potion.
Since centuries she had remained the same.
She neither eats nor drinks,
Yet hums the love songs
incessantly.
Everyone is puzzled
and curious to know
Is she a fairy or a yogini?
Who remains perpetually
in trance all day through.
It seems she is enamoured
by the love of Almighty.
Her soul is entwined
with divinity.
She is perhaps the

Radha of Krishna

Whose love was spiritual.
We mortals are engrossed
in mundane life.
But the exalted souls
who are enamoured by God
Are indeed immortalised.

Ode to Unrequited Love

Oh! You cruel unrequited love.
Have you ever realised?
You encompass so much,
Misery and heartbreak.
I am amazed and aghast.
To watch how you play,
with people's lives.
Just like a potter who churns out,
New earthenware each night.
Oh! Unrequited love.
Is your callousness deliberate?
Or are you just complacent?
Alas! If only you could reciprocate.
There would be thousands of
Happy faces which
You -could create.
It becomes difficult for me to fathom,
Why do people pine for thee!
One who is listless and devoid of all emotions.
You who cannot even comprehend

How to accept love,
Which is pure and simple.
Oh! Unrequited love.
You who roam about unnamed and masked.
Has managed to somehow survive.
On folly and trust of
Innocent hearts and minds.
I admonish and implore thee.
To at least come forward and
get out of your self
imposed exile,
And inflated ego.
I hereby challenged thee.
To at least try once.
And feel the sweet
fragrance of love.
I know it is onerous to
confront the onslaught
Of love.
To stall the deluge of emotions.
Oh! Unrequited love.
I do understand your ambivalence.
Your reasons for being confounded.
But even then, I request thee To hear the
Soulful music of love.
Don't be irreverent
To something

Which is the expression
Of God's divinity.
I assure you
Oh! Unrequited love
You will soon realise
This is your epiphany.

Martyrs

My salute to martyrs.
The listless eyes and pale faces,
Haunt me.
The news trickles every day.
About one more soldier's demise.
I am distraught.
The nation salutes the martyrs.
But it pains me to accept the fact
Young bubbling lives full of laughter and pride
Are being killed by disgruntled forces outright.
They, who were the apple of their parent's eyes
Fought bravely and died.
Was it their destiny, or
we are responsible
who are vying for hegemony?
There are stories of many remote villages
where now exists
Lone parents, widows, and kids.
Most of the boys
have not come back home.

For they, while
Fighting the enemy, were
martyred for motherland.
When will this mayhem and cacophony end?
Has history not taught us enough lessons?
It is said even
after the epic war of Mahabharat,
None survived except the Pandavas
To celebrate the victory
And bask in its glory.
It seems futile to blow
your trumpets.
As no one has permanence.
However, with all grace and humbleness
I salute the brave sons of soil.
And offer my heart full condolences,
To equally worthy
and brave family members.

The Tamarind Tree

As I sat on my favourite chair.
On a lazy Sunday afternoon,
The combo of
The retreating Sun,
Showering its warm rays, and
the lullaby of the fragrance filled cool fluttering breeze,
Was too attractive to resist.
The ethereal comfort and quite
Soothed my tired nerves.
And compelled me to doze off for a while.
I found myself sitting under the
Old Tamarind tree.
Was I day dreaming or was it real?
Suddenly like a flash of lightning,
I was transported on to an old memory lane.
I stood before my old house.
And saw the old Tamarind tree that stood erect since a
century. I recognised my old friends.
Small pretty girls with pink faces.
I saw their coloured frocks and
heard excited voices.

Their hands and feet covered with mosses.
This had a cascading effect.
I remembered the days when my parents took an afternoon siesta.
And how I would sneak out from my house stealthy.
This indeed was my secret mission.
To be with my tree friend,
The big and majestic Tamarind.
We little girls would pick our treasures.
Elated to collect those tangy fruit and leaves.
There were altogether five row houses
And five tamarind trees.
There were variety of birds and their nests.
An old python
As it was said
Sleeping since ages under its bed.
I abruptly woke up from my slumber,
Hearing the shrill cry of the crow,
my cranky old friend.
Who, sitting aggressively on my window sill,
Was enquiring about my dream.
I suddenly realised it was a nostalgic trip.
To meet my old pal, the Tamarind.
Who I found had gone long ago.
With the advent of metro station.
Is it not ironical?
For making more place for ourselves,
We are cutting short the lives of others.

Ode to Sleep

Oh, dear sleep!
Why do you elude me?
You, who is resplendent,
With moonlight and glittering stars.
You, who is alluring and full of grace.
Brimming with life's force.
Oh sleep!
Don't bother about my gabbling.
It is not a cry of damsel in distress.
Nevertheless, I seriously feel,
You are a little hard with me.
You keep a watch on me.
Like an old headmistress.
Oh, dear sleep!
Why do you elude me?
I am perplexed,
With your enigmatic smile.
Your silhouette looks like an
unguent of calm and quite.
Your silence bestows mankind

With serenity and fills everyone with soulful music.
So, I ask thee humbly,
Oh sleep!
Why do you elude me?
I ponder about those times,
When I was young and in my prime.
You were always by my side.
But I find,
As I am becoming forlorn and hazy,
You have started playing mischief.
I earnestly ask for your benevolence,
With folded hands.
Oh, dear sleep!
Come to my rescue.
Remove the web of darkness and fear.
Help me weave new dreams.
Unlimited and fair.
Rejuvenate me.
So that I can carry forward,
Oh: The torch of faith and bliss.
Remove the dark demons of hatred and mistrust that chase me. Help me to preserve,
All that is beautiful.
Allow me to offer my gratitude,
To the Supreme.
But only if,
Oh sleep!
You come to my rescue.

Uninterrupted.
And for once,
Stop eluding me.

Hope

I get up from my slumber,
With a renewed hope,
I will start living my dreams.
I hope henceforth no one will be
able to debilitate my resolve.
I try my best not to give ear to anything preposterous.
I hope I will stop condoning the slow demise of my consciousness.
But alas in vain!
As the day progresses,
I find myself deeply entrenched,
In a web of myriad false promises.
I am fully aware that death of physical being leads to salvation. But this slow death of my fiery spirits,
Has become almost a drudgery.
I continue making compromises,
For fear of reprisals.
This unending load on my heart,
Has become too voluminous to endure any more.
I hope my epiphany will appear soon.

It will tear the shackles of fear and servitude.
But I know now.
I cannot have hope of hope.
It is me who has to stand upright,
I have to become fearless of all that is dark and sinister,
I have to get out of this agony and excruciating pain,
And illuminate my soul.
I hope to do it soon.

The Sea and Me

While watching the Sea,
Which looked calm and serene
I felt it resembles me.
Some days I am more peaceful.
And some days the ghosts of past,
and present, unequivocally disturb me.
It seems you are also ambivalent,
h:And behave alternately like me.
I sit before you Oh Sea!
You are irreverent and inexorable.
I am confounded and wonder
What are you murmuring?
I had seen you whistling and dancing.
But some days you become too formal.
Are you also juggling and wrestling,
To find the answers of your existence?
As I too do often.
I behold you Oh Sea!
To find the answers and tell me.
I am aware you are flowing since eternity.

Are you also tired of treading the same path,
Of flowing continuously?
Or have you accepted this as your destiny?
Does this acceptance make you more peaceful,
As it has made me?

The Clouds

It seems as if the clouds have
Ensconced themselves in the sky.
Have they come with full force to stay a while?
The intermittent rain drops are making a peculiar noise.
The trees have become lush green and so have the brown mountains. Everywhere there is water.
Small rivulets are running around laughing and playing pranks.
I heard a distant cry of a flying bird.
Sitting at my balcony,
It seems I am in a dream.
The clouds appear to be fully dressed.
As if arrived for some
Special occasion.
But sometimes their countenance appears to me quite strange. As if they are raving about some souls unknown.
I pray thee to remain amiable.
Not to wreak havoc.
You are the life force of this Earth.
Have always been welcomed with open hearts by all of us.

So don't destroy what is sweet and
Simple,
With your over indulgence.

May I Be

I wish to be a singing bird.
Full of melodious songs for all ears.
I wish to be audible to all faiths, castes, creeds, and races.
I wish to sing a song for all beings depressed and elated.
I wish to sing a verse for all kings and their subjects.
May my lullaby help them forget all bloodshed.
My songs will be for all those who don't use their vision to see this beautiful universe.
I wish to tune a special melody for all those
Who are filled with hate and misogyny in their minds,
Who treat mankind as if it is meant to be oppressed.
I wish to sit and fly on a dragonfly's back.
Humming and singing near the pure and serene waterfall.
I wish to be a tree full of flowers and scents
Which goes inside the nostrils and fills the souls
With joy and happiness.
I wish to transcend oceans and rivers, forests and the sky.
If only my wish comes true and
I can fly.

My Journey

What is my journey?
I often ask.
Nothing great. Just rudimentary.
My existence is like a particle of sand in this vast universe.
With passage of time my footprints will be gone forever.
All people close to me have faded from my reminiscence.
What purpose have I served?
I know not.
Childhood was happy, adulthood strange.
All have hastened their pace.
I met no sages.
I encountered no God.
Though my search continued.
My soul guided, my mind misled.
It was a continuous battle of good winning over the evil within me. I wanted wings to soar high.
I was pulled back to this Earth
where finally I will mingle as and when I die.
The folly of attaining greatness stares blankly
As one closes its karmic account.

The struggles, the desires, the envies, the ego,
All are battered by death, which sings an ominous note.
But it is in fact a welcome change from servitude to living free.
The storms are full of dust.
The sky is blurred.
But the ticking rain is a hope of rest and peace.

Who ?

It is not me, it is only You.
It is not they, it is only You.
It is not we, it is only You.
What is that
I wish to conquer?
I wish to control?
I wish to surrender?
It is not easy.
It takes years to understand.
It is at the end of one's journey
That one realises
The greatest hurdle is one's ego.
False hopes, false promises.
It is this bridge which I try to cross.
My hand is about to touch
Thee! O! My Lord.
My endeavour to seek you
If only you help!

●●●

BLACK EAGLE BOOKS

www.blackeaglebooks.org
info@blackeaglebooks.org

Black Eagle Books, an independent publisher, was founded as a nonprofit organization in April, 2019. It is our mission to connect and engage the Indian diaspora and the world at large with the best of works of world literature published on a collaborative platform, with special emphasis on foregrounding Contemporary Classics and New Writing.

www.ingramcontent.com/pod-product-compliance
Lightning Source LLC
Chambersburg PA
CBHW030534080526
44585CB00014B/945